Animal Parents

Written by Lee Wang
Series Consultant: Linda Hoyt

WorldWise
Content-based Learning

Contents

Introduction

Emperor penguin baby

All adult animals are able to produce young animals. They work very hard to make sure that their offspring have the best chance to grow up and **reproduce**, too. In this way, the species survives.

Numbat mother carrying babies on her back

A mother robin feeds her babies.

Some animals, such as opossums, take care of their young for a long time after they are born or hatch. They provide food, protect them, and teach them what they need to know to survive.

Because this is a lot of hard work, these parents usually have very few babies.

Baby stinkbugs

Baby sea turtle

Find out more

Two Australian mammals lay eggs instead of giving birth to live young. Can you find the names of these animals?

Other animals, such as bugs and spiders, lay hundreds or thousands of eggs, and they leave the eggs to hatch. They do not stay to care for the eggs or the young animals after they hatch. The parents lay these eggs in places where the hatchlings can easily find food.

They lay lots of eggs because when these young animals hatch, there are many **predators** that want to eat them. Only a few survive to grow into adults and reproduce.

What do all these animal parents have in common?

Butterflies and caterpillars

5

Chapter 1

Mammal families

Young mammals are much smaller than their parents. They need their mother's milk to help them grow. Often, they are born blind and without fur on their skins.

Most female mammals give birth to one to three young because a lot of time and energy is needed to feed and protect them. When larger numbers of young mammals are born, other family members usually help out.

Mammal	Typical number of young	Length of time fed on mother's milk	Who protects and teaches the young?
Koala	1	1 year, but they start to eat other food at 6 months	The female koala
Grey wolf	7	10 weeks, but they also eat meat brought to them by pack members	Both parents and other members of the family pack
Beaver	9	4 months, but they also eat plants brought to them by other family members	Both parents and other family members

Koala

Thirty-five days after mating, the female koala gives birth to one joey and raises it by herself. The young koala looks like a pink jellybean. It is only two centimetres long. It crawls into a pouch on the mother's stomach and feeds on her milk.

The joey grows slowly and gets fur. After six months, it also eats its mother's runny droppings called "pap". At seven months old, the joey leaves the pouch for longer periods of time and rides on its mother's back as she moves around the tree. It starts to eat gum leaves as well as drinking her milk.

The joey stays with its mother for up to two years. After this, it moves to its own trees to feed on leaves.

A mother koala and its baby joey. Koalas have one baby called a joey.

A joey

A joey in its mother's pouch

Grey wolf

The female grey wolf carries her young inside her body for nine weeks. She gives birth to about seven pups in a den. The pups feed on their mother's milk for ten weeks and grow quickly.

During this time, other wolves in the pack hunt for meat. They take some of this meat to the den for the mother. They also bring up some of this meat from their stomachs for the pups to eat. This is called **regurgitating**.

When the pups are able to leave the den, some of the wolves in the pack guard them from **predators** while others go hunting.

When they are six months old, the pups leave the den for the last time and join the pack. Wolves continue to work together in packs over their lifetime to find and share food.

A member of the pack is on guard to protect a wolf pup.

A wolf feeds her cubs with food she has regurgitated.

Beaver

Beavers live together in a lodge under the water in a river. They use sticks to build the lodge.

The female beaver carries her young inside her body for 15 weeks. She gives birth to about nine baby beavers, which are called kits. The mother feeds her kits milk for up to four months.

Kits can swim from the time they are born. They can carry and chew food underwater. All members of the family group help care for the kits. The kits live with their families for years before leaving to start families of their own.

Young beavers feeding on leaves

Baby beavers in a lodge.

Find out more

The female orangutan usually has only one baby at a time. She looks after her baby longer than any other animal (except humans). How long does she care for it? What does she teach it during this time? Which other large mammals usually have only one offspring at a time?

Chapter 2

Parent birds

All female birds lay eggs. The young birds grow inside the eggs. The mother or father sits on these eggs to keep them warm and safe.

When the young birds hatch, they are naked, blind and helpless. They need to be fed and protected for quite some time.

Bird	Typical number of young	Incubation of eggs	Care of young
Emperor penguin	1	Male parent takes care of the egg for about 64 days	Both parents feed the chick for approximately 120 days
White-bellied sea eagle	1–3	Both parents share the task for about 35 days	Both parents feed the chick for up to 10 to 11 weeks
Laughing kookaburra	3	Both parents and other family members share the task for about 24 days	Parents and other family members bring food for about 10 weeks and help raise the young for about 3 years

A young chick is fed by one
of its parents.

Did you know?
If the female Emperor penguin
returns late from hunting, the
male can feed the chick with
a type of rich milk he makes
in his throat.

Emperor penguin

The female Emperor penguin lays one egg
on sea ice at the start of winter in Antarctica.
The male penguin looks after the egg while
the female goes to sea to hunt for fish.

All the male penguins huddle together in large
groups to stay warm. Each male stands upright
for about 64 days, protecting the egg that rests
on his feet in a pouch of belly skin. He loses
half his body weight while **incubating** the egg.

The female returns when the chick hatches,
and she feeds it with fish that she brings up or
regurgitates from her stomach. She takes over
caring for the chick while the male goes out to
sea to hunt for fish and rebuild his body weight.

When the male returns, both parents care for
the chick. When the chick is about 120 days
old, it is ready to go to sea to find food.

Male Emperor penguins huddle
together to stay warm.

11

The nest of the white-bellied sea eagle

Find out more

Do you know other birds that look after their young for a long time? Make a list to share.

White-bellied sea eagle

White-bellied sea eagles build nests in very tall trees for the female to lay her eggs. The female sea eagle lays between one and three eggs at a time. The male not only helps the female build the nest, but he also shares the task of sitting on the nest to **incubate** the eggs for 35 days to keep them warm.

When one bird is on the nest, the other goes off to find food. Sea eagles hunt fish, reptiles, birds and mammals. After the chicks hatch, both parents share feeding them for 10 to 11 weeks before the young leave the nest to hunt for food by themselves.

A white-bellied sea eagle

Laughing kookaburra

Laughing kookaburras live in family groups of about seven. Each family has male and female adult kookaburras and their young from the past five years.

All the adult kookaburras work together to make a nest in a tree hollow. The female lays about three eggs in this nest. The adult male and female and the younger birds take turns to incubate these eggs for up to 24 days.

When the chicks hatch, the parents and the other family members feed them for over 10 weeks. All the family members help raise the young kookaburras for a few years before leaving to find a mate and make their own nest.

Baby kookaburras

Did you know?

Ostriches nest on the ground. They lay a large number of eggs, which they need to guard from **predators**. The hatchlings have feathers, and they can walk and run quickly and feed themselves. But they still need protection from a parent.

A couple of kookaburras

An ostrich guarding its eggs

13

Chapter 3

Saltwater fish families

Female saltwater fish need to lay lots of eggs to make sure a few of their young fish survive. After the young hatch, they have to look after themselves and find food in the sea. The young fish are tiny, and some can die when the strong ocean currents wash them away.

The young fish are also easy to hunt. Other sea creatures can easily catch and eat them.

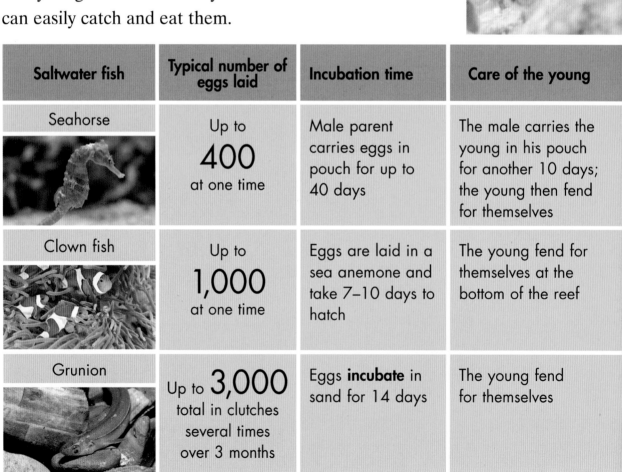

Saltwater fish	Typical number of eggs laid	Incubation time	Care of the young
Seahorse	Up to **400** at one time	Male parent carries eggs in pouch for up to 40 days	The male carries the young in his pouch for another 10 days; the young then fend for themselves
Clown fish	Up to **1,000** at one time	Eggs are laid in a sea anemone and take 7–10 days to hatch	The young fend for themselves at the bottom of the reef
Grunion	Up to **3,000** total in clutches several times over 3 months	Eggs **incubate** in sand for 14 days	The young fend for themselves

Seahorse

The female seahorse lays between 250 and 400 eggs. She transfers the eggs in small batches to the male's pouch. He carries them in his pouch for three to six weeks. He does not eat during this time.

When the young seahorses hatch, the male carries them in his pouch for another ten days until they are about six millimetres long. He then ejects them into the seawater.

The young seahorses must take care of themselves. They eat tiny pieces of plankton in the seawater and try to stay away from **predators** such as crabs, fish and stingrays.

This male seahorse has young seahorses in his bulging pouch.

This baby seahorse is two weeks old. At this stage, you can see its digestive system. The small animals it feeds on give this seahorse an orange colour.

Clown fish in a sea anemone

Clown fish

Clown fish parents work together to make a nursery in a sea anemone. The female lays up to 1,000 eggs at a time and the male **fertilises** them. Both parents look after the eggs. They wave their fins over the eggs to provide a constant supply of water filled with oxygen to keep the eggs alive.

Once the young clown fish hatch, they must swim and look after themselves. They feed on leftover fish that have been caught by the anemone. They hide inside the anemone's **tentacles** to avoid predators such as sharks and stingrays.

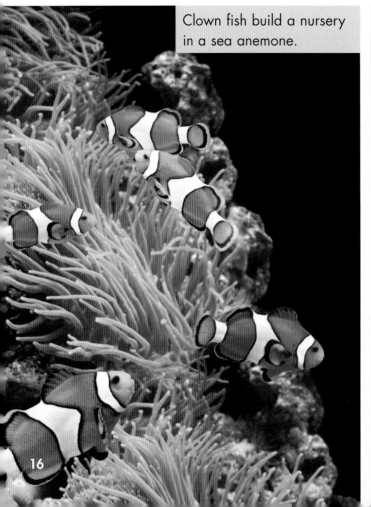

Clown fish build a nursery in a sea anemone.

A clown fish parent looks after the eggs.

Grunion

Unlike other fish, grunion lay their eggs in the sand on beaches. This happens during the full moon, when tens of thousands of grunion come ashore with the tide.

Each female makes a hole in the sand with her tail. She lays about 3,000 eggs that are then fertilised by the male. Both parents return to the sea and the fertilised eggs remain safe in the sand.

After 14 days, the young fish hatch and are washed out to sea by the waves. The young eat small plants and animals and look after themselves in the sea. Many young grunion do not survive because other fish hunt them.

A full moon

Grunion eggs

A female grunion lays her eggs in sand on a beach, and a male grunion fertilises them.

Chapter 4

Other animal parents

While some animals do not look after their young, they try to protect their eggs by covering or enclosing them with different materials. When the young hatch from these eggs, they have to look after themselves.

Amphibians

Frogs, toads, salamanders and some other animals that live in water lay their eggs in freshwater. A clear case of jelly develops around the eggs to protect them. The eggs hatch into young larvae that grow quickly. Their bodies change, and they become adults.

Find out more

Poison dart frogs have unusual ways of looking after their young. Find out what the male does after the female lays her eggs.

Cane toads

Female cane toads lay up to 35,000 eggs in a few seconds. The male quickly **fertilises** these eggs. Neither parent stays to take care of the eggs or the tadpoles.

Baby turtles try to make it back to the sea before a predator catches them.

Find out more

Unlike most other reptiles, female rattlesnakes do not lay their eggs. The eggs hatch inside the female's body. Does the mother look after them after they are born?

Reptiles

Female snakes, lizards, turtles and many other reptiles lay eggs. They dig a hole or burrow, lay their eggs and cover them with sand or dirt. This keeps the eggs warm until the young hatch. Some reptiles have live young.

Sea turtles

Female sea turtles haul themselves onto a beach, dig a large hole and lay up to 200 eggs in it at one time. They cover these eggs with sand and then return to the sea. They repeat this nesting and egg-laying task up to eight times in a breeding season.

When the young turtles hatch, they have to scramble over the sand to the sea. Not all of them make it. The sea also has many **predators** that eat these young turtles, so only a few survive.

Green sea turtles come ashore to lay eggs.

19

Spiders

All female spiders lay a large number of eggs. They weave a silk egg sac to protect them. Most leave the egg sac, but some female spiders carry it with them to take care of it. Many young spiders do not survive. They become food for birds, reptiles and wasps.

The wolf spider

After she has mated, the female wolf spider weaves a mat of silk and lays 100 or more eggs on it. She then weaves silk around the eggs, draws up the sides of the mat, and sews it together with silk to make a ball. She attaches the egg sac under her body with silk and carries it with her for about 28 days.

When the young spiders hatch, they crawl onto their mother's back and cling to hairs. She carries them around for about 14 days to protect them. They do not need food or water during this time.

A female wolf spider with an egg sac

When the young spiders hatch, they climb onto their mother's back.

Insects

The female of insects such as butterflies, ants and beetles lay a large number of eggs but only a few of their young survive to become adults. A few insects such as aphids give birth to live young.

Butterflies lay their eggs on or near the plants that their young can feed on.

An Australian eastern swallowtail butterfly (above) and caterpillar (below).

Australian eastern swallowtail butterfly

The female usually lays up to 400 eggs on the upperside of leaves or on stems. She then flies off and leaves the eggs.

When the larvae hatch after seven to ten days, they feed on these plants. They eat for three to four weeks.

Each one then spins a case called a pupa and rests inside for up to six months. The pupa opens and a butterfly emerges.

Life cycle of a butterfly

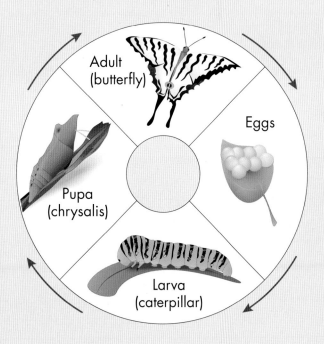

Adult (butterfly)

Eggs

Larva (caterpillar)

Pupa (chrysalis)

Conclusion

Baby animals are either born live or hatch from eggs. They all need food to help them grow. Some animal parents provide food for them when they are very young. They might do this separately or together, or have other adult animals or family members help out.

Some animals take care of their offspring for a long time. They teach them to look for food, to build shelters and to escape **predators**. Other animals find a safe place to lay their eggs or to have their live young so that their young can look after themselves.

There are many ways in which animals raise their young. What they all have in common is that the adults try to give their offspring the best chance of surviving so they too can **reproduce**.

Glossary

fertilise — to make an egg able to grow

incubate — to hatch eggs by keeping them warm

predator — an animal that hunts other animals

regurgitate — to bring food that has been swallowed back up to the mouth

reproduce — to have babies

tentacles — long snake-like arms

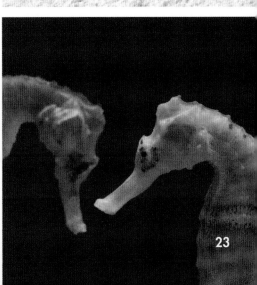

Index